NOBODY HAS A PERFECT HUSBAND

JEET BRAR

ISBN 979-888521636-4

Dedictaed to my husband whom

I can never thank enough

for his motivation, love and support

Contents

CHAPTER I

Tick Tock Tick

In my childhood days, Mehta uncle lived in our society. We kids really adored him because he was not only a very jolly person, but he would also play with us nearly every evening. Those were the golden days when even private employees were home by six in the evening. The moment he walked into our society at the stroke of six, we started running towards him to show our affection. He would also acknowledge our cheers and leave us with the promise that he would return soon to play with us. However, it was a sort of a ritual that after Mehta uncle came to play with us, after an hour or so, his wife would come. Then they would leave for the market or nearby park to spend their evening.

It so happened one day that while playing Mehta, uncle's shirt got dirty with mud, and at that exact moment, his wife came out to go for their usual evening stroll. Mehta uncle smiled at her and told her to wait for some time to change his shirt. This irked the lady so much that she shouted at Mehta uncle for always making excuses and getting them late for the evening outings. Needless to say, we all were surprised. Aunty kept yelling at him for some other mistakes that he had committed in the past or perhaps didn't commit. It was very much visible from uncle's face that it didn't go too well with him. He yelled back at her and said that he waits for her every day and passed his time with the children so that she could get ready, but on that one day, she couldn't wait for him for even five minutes. The fight escalated, and both the husband-wife kept arguing in a high-pitched voice until some neighborhood aunties intervened. I remember that was the last day Mehta uncle had played with us.

After that day, something had changed in their relationship. We still ran towards Mehta uncle gleefully when he returned from his office, and he acknowledged our welcome, but he never came back again to the playing field. Neither he and his wife went for their evening stroll. Most of the time, Mehta uncle only used to go out in the evening to buy daily necessities. The fight which the couple had publically left a deep effect on their marriage.However, after I grew up, I realized that Mehta uncle's fight with his wife was long pending. His wife would make him wait every day. He is a good-natured man who didn't make a big issue of it. Still, when that day she laid the blame on him publically in front of the very children in whose eyes he was nothing less than a hero, Uncle reached the limit of his patience. I always remembered this incident, and whenever I saw mellowed-down Mehta uncle, I felt sorry for him. I learned two life lessons from this incident: never keep the other person waiting(especially your husband); secondly, don't take another person for granted. Sometimes our little habits lead to huge ugly consequences.

Eighty percent of fights amongst married couples are because of time management. In some cases, it's the husband who doesn't value time, and in some, the wife takes punctuality for a ride. Needless to say, the other person and the entire family suffer due to one person's habits. Suppose the wife can't complete her chores on time. In that case, the kid and the husband are late for school and office, respectively. Their day is already ruined due to the high-stress level they experience while setting out to work. They start their day with negative emotions, and they blame it all on the woman of the house. Subconsciously they start losing respect for her. They are filled with rage for her though they themselves are not fully aware of why they don't like her too much. On the other hand, the woman fails to understand where she is wrong in her relationships. The silent devil here is time.

In the initial days of our marriage, we had this habit of going out for a walk after having our dinner. We always made it a point to have our dinner before 8:30 PM. Now there was a colleague of my husband whom we often met on our after-dinner walks. We used to have a normal tet-e-tete with him, and once or twice we asked him casually whether his dinner was over. He seemed a bit surprised at first that we dined so early and made an excuse that the dinner at his house was late. However, one day when we asked him the same question as an icebreaker, he replied a bit remorsefully to my husband that everybody isn't lucky to have dinner ready on time every day. While saying so, he lowered his head, and we felt very sad for him. We didn't think much about asking him the same casual question often, but he was having difficulty answering us. After coming from the office in the evening, we noticed that he often sat in the park until dinner was ready, sometimes till 10PM. As understood, his wife used to prepare dinner too late, and the poor fellow, though he wanted to eat early and rest, failed to do so.

I often thought how come his wife didn't think about keeping the dinner ready early or spending quality time with him in the evening rather than spending every evening of her life in the kitchen.In contrast, he spent his time waiting for a basic thing like dinner. However, I know some women just can't change their habits. Some women are always late; on the contrary, we also have women who are always ready early. For example, one of my friends wakes up and cooks lunch before 8 AM every day. I asked her why she makes lunch in the morning when her husband comes home every day for lunch. It's not that he used to take his lunchbox to the office to this she replied, "It's too hot to cook in the afternoon besides I like to finish my work and watch television undisturbed. " I just went quiet but thought about her poor husband and children who have to eat sort of stale food in the afternoon just because mommy dear likes to finish her all kitchen work in one shot.

So what's the way out? If you want to have a more peaceful existence with your husband, respect his time. Try to get ready at the given time, keep the food ready, and pay the bills on time. Most importantly, spend quality time with him. Don't impose your routine on him. Give him his time and space. If he doesn't have time for you because of being genuinely busy, try to manage your life independently. There is no use in complaining about things which can't be changed due to practical reasons. Constantly complaining to him that he doesn't give time to you will only make you look like a clingy wife. However, it's okay to demand some time from him for yourself if he is intentionally not giving you much time. These little changes in your habits and routine will bring more happiness and peace to your married life. As they say, time respects those who respect time; in this case, the husband respects her who respects his time.

CHAPTER II

Gender Battles

I have attended many conferences and seminars in my career. An unforgettable incident occurred at one such very high profile conference that changed my outlook towards being a working woman by 360 degrees. In that particular conference, the highly placed IAS officers of our country were participating. I knew one woman IAS who was working in a very high-profile position. We had sort of friendly relations with each other. Frankly speaking, I was in awe of her because of her position. It so happened that when we met during the lunch hour, we started talking casually like we always did. On all the previous occasions, we chatted mostly about various cultural or current affairs.

However, that day my friend seemed a bit distracted. I politely inquired if everything was alright. On this, she just let go of her professional image and started telling me how she was distraught because her maid had left her. She went on to tell me that she was staying along with both her kids only as her husband, who was also an IAS, was posted in another city. After the maid left, the entire household was a mess, and she was struggling to manage both home and office. While she was sharing her problems with me, I listened to her with my eyes wide open. I couldn't believe that a woman like her, who was powerful, had to worry about such mundane stuff. Whenever I saw her with her security guards and drivers, I always imagined her as someone who just concentrated on her official work and trained servants to take care of her household and other chores. However, her disclosure shattered that image. The biggest reality that hit me hard was that it's always our responsibility to look after the house and kids in India, no matter what position we women reach.

The life of a married working woman in India is a dog's life. Around ninety percent of the working women in our country, whether they are poor labourers or at a high profile job, have to do household chores before leaving for office and are welcomed back by the same. Once back, they walk straight into the kitchen to make a cup of tea for themselves, cook dinner, look after the kids' studies, do laundry, wash dishes, make preparations for the next day, and whatnot. Ask any homemaker how her life is, and she will reply she slogs the whole day. The same is true about the working woman who just adds ten hours of outside work to all homemakers' duties. So much for women's equality and liberation. What is the point of such liberty and equality if it's at the expense of back-breaking hard work day in and day out along with the mental stress of a job and family life? This is not freedom or a good life for a woman; it's just a no man's land where the woman just couldn't have the best of both worlds. I know many women have made it big. Neither am I saying that women should not venture into jobs or business. Still, then women must be ready for some cruel realities and not expect a rosy pinky picture of being a working woman after marriage from the beginning because that only can help them to live such a life, or they will be more frustrated than happy with their life.

We all know that Indian society is a male-dominated one. In our country, men and women are divided into typical gender roles. However, whereas Indian women's role has undergone a marked change, sadly, the Indian men are still stuck in the age-old gender role. Indian men and women both go out to work these days, but only the women have to take care of the household. The Indian man enjoys the benefit of double income, but he doesn't want to share the responsibilities which come along with it. Indian men hardly help women when it comes to household chores as they consider it shameful to do so. The patriarchal setup of the society has ingrained in the minds of the Indian men that doing household chores is primarily a woman's work, and it's non-macho to enter the kitchen.

During the recent Corona pandemic, we all witnessed men cooking in the kitchen once or twice and uploading their photos on social media to showcase their uber cool and sensitive nature towards their wives. However, we all know the truth. So what's the way out. Now there are three ways to deal with this problem. Firstly understand there is no use in crying over split milk. I know many women who get frustrated by their husband's behavior and keep quarreling with him to give a helping hand with the children or the household work.

In some cases, it works, but there are just more fights and bad blood in most others. To my friends who are stuck in this situation, I would like to suggest that lady, you have sealed the deal with the devil now there is no point to fight with him. I mean, we all know what we are getting into when we marry a person. We know whether he will be helping us with our life or just behaving like a male chauvinist. I mean, if we know that a man can't cook, then we can't expect him to become a chef overnight. We are aware of the kind of family he is raised in, so don't expect miracles. You may try to change him, but it will work only to an extent so try to accept the reality and attain mental peace rather than making your house a battlefield or feeling angry about the situation. Trust me, constantly expecting him to help you will just soak your energy like a sponge, and whatever is left of you will also be at risk of breaking down.Now the first way leads to the second path, which is before you marry, choose the guy carefully. Be sure what type of guy you are looking for. Look at his family, enquire whether he can cook or do household chores. The person who helps his mom in the kitchen will also help you. So set your goals straight before marriage though it's kind of a situation reversal with you asking the groom can he cook or do household work.

The third way to make your life better is to leave the job or the marriage. Your family can't have the cake and keep it too. If they want to enjoy the perks of your income, they must also give a hand with the responsibilities. However, if you are doing the job just to prove yourself as a liberal, educated woman, you are burning yourself out. Darling, I would suggest you stop and consider. Is this really what you want? Is it really worth it? If it's not ok and if financially you can leave the job, it's better to leave the job, find some creative interest, and enjoy yourself rather than breaking under the pressure of handling both the world's together. If you don't want to leave the job but think that your partner's behavior should change, look for a better option. Don't take too much pressure. In the end, no one values your hard work or sacrifices, but you might hear from your own children that you were never around for them. So think and act wisely. Just challenging and fighting the gender battle won't serve any purpose. It's time to make tough decisions.

Now totally opposite to these working women, some homemakers are masters of the gender game. These women have a habit of constant nagging. These ladies, I am sorry to say, are continuously fighting with their husbands. I know some women who are all happy go lucky when the husband is in office, but the moment he returns, they start behaving as if they are the busiest people on the earth or are in some sort of pain or children are after their lives, in short, they create a tensed hyperactive type of ambiance in the house and start demanding their husband to help them with the household work or go for grocery shopping or do this or that.

All in all, they can't see their husbands happy and relaxed in the house. They might be sitting and watching the television for hours while the husband is slogging in the office, but they time all their chores so that when the man returns home, he should get an impression that the woman is busy working all day long. Most of the time, these women haven't done any job themselves and fail to understand how difficult it is to actually do a job and not commit a mistake because that will mean taking the family down with you. It seems like they imagine their husband's job is equivalent to lying down on the water bed in the office. You will often hear these ladies saying, "my husband is lucky just leaves for office in the morning and returns at night. I am the one who has to face the music of household duties".

Some of these ladies are like out to avenge something when it comes to their husbands. Since I have been on both sides of the fence as a working woman and as well a homemaker, I can tell you that being a homemaker is much, much easier than being a working woman and even if you are just working without the household responsibilities, doing a job is not easy in India where an average person spends twelve hours of the day around their job. I feel pity for the husbands who have such wives because these poor souls don't even have a home to relax. I mean, just because I am a woman shouldn't make me partial towards my clan, isn't it?

Now it's mainly this category of homemakers who also sow seeds of gender discrimination in their families by making their sons spoilt brats and typifying their daughters into the age-old role of homemakers viz learning to cook, clean, and other things. Suppose we want our daughters to really lead a balanced life where they can manage their professional and personal lives comfortably. In that case, we must teach our sons the household chores just as we teach our daughters everything about managing the house. We must teach our sons that there is no discrimination related to work. Every work is important, and there is nothing like a man's job or a woman's job. We should also teach our sons that there is no need to stick to a stereotypical image of a man but become a man who has many different aspects to his personality. It is only by doing so that we may be assured that in the future, we can build a more gender-neutral society than the one in which we are living currently.

CHAPTER III

A Little Bit of Romance

My living room was bathed in the golden morning sun, and I had settled down comfortably on my sofa to have my morning tea. In front of me on the huge TV screen, a beautiful song was playing. The hero and the heroine were walking hand in hand amidst beautiful scenic locales singing their hearts out to confess their love towards each other. As the song progresses, the scene shifts to a marketplace where the hero lovingly teases the heroine and then chases her till she happily gives up her futile struggle. Such a happy couple, enjoying their holidays in such a romantic way, thought my poor heart and my brain started comparing my own vacation experiences with that of the on-screen couple. It's not that we as a couple didn't enjoy our holidays or didn't do fun things, but what chance does our common man vacations stand in Front of such highly expressive Bollywood ones. I am sure our holidays will fall flat-faced on the ground when compared to these Bollywood songs. Before marriage, every girl thinks that violins will start playing automatically on her vacation and she will be dancing on the clouds after marriage. However, it's only after marriage that we realize that maybe our husband will run away from the very place where someone is actually playing the violin, labeling it as cacophony. So much for the violins, my friend. Rest in peace, violin *wala* romance.

It's sad to accept, but the truth is Indian husbands are the most unromantic ones on the global index. Now you would say, what are you saying? Don't you see the

Instagram posts of romantic grooms dancing for their wives on the wedding day or proposing to her before the marriage in Paris? Now, hold your horses. Ten husbands hardly even smile for their own wedding photos in India when compared to that one romantic husband. Don't trust me? Check the very insta which you vouch for, and you can see photos of grooms standing with their wives as if they need to go to the loo as soon as the photo session is over. Besides, today's idea of romance is highly influenced or may have originated from what the western world has taught us. The candlelight dinners, the bouquet of roses, chocolates, Valentine's Day, and all the other mushy mushy things are western, so what were Indian men doing to express their romantic side? Maybe bringing *gajra* was the highest gesture of romance for the Indian man.

I mean, how many of us have visited a proper honeymoon destination like Switzerland, Paris, Goa, or Kerala straight after the marriage, and how many of us have gone to pay our respects to our respective Kul devis and devtas. I am sure the ones who have gone to chant 'Jai Mata Di' are more than those who went to destination honeymoons. Even if we Indians go on a honeymoon, it's mostly for a day or two, and that's it. So much for the much-awaited romantic honeymoon, which we keep planning throughout our unmarried lives. In India, from the day we are married, we listen to the dialogue, 'you have your whole life for love, do something worthwhile in your youth' and our husbands take this advice so seriously that half of them leave the newly wed bride high and dry to join their respective jobs. The remaining half look at it irresponsible to enjoy with their wives and choose sitting on 'papa's *galla*' instead.

However, it's better to be rational in this matter. Now Some newly wed brides have their heads so full of the idea of the romantic marriage and those stupid filmy songs that they believe that their marriage is a failure if the husband doesn't pamper them like a Bollywood hero. They want to live in their la-la land forever and don't want to face the realities of life. They keep pestering their husbands to spend more time with them, which creates more rifts rather than bringing the couple closer to each other. The innocent, loving wife transforms into a nagging wife overnight for the husband. Many a times, it also happens that the husband tries to please the wife in his romantic way, but the wife doesn't have the same idea of romance as the husband. One of my friend's husbands took her on a month-long vacation as a surprise immediately after their marriage. Now you would be like, wow! There comes the heartthrob but trust me, and you wouldn't like to be on such a vacation. The husband took her trekking into some remote jungle. He thought spending time alone in those tent houses was extremely romantic, but ask my friend, and she would say those were the worst day of her life. She is a city girl, and staying in those tents without air-conditioning or other basic facilities was nothing less than torture for her. Needless to say that they returned after a week or so with complaint boxes.

Everyone has a different romantic bone. Whereas some ladies love to go shopping with their husbands, others would prefer to go to a movie. Some women may like to go on dinner dates, while others would love to go on long drives. Everyone's definition of romance is different. So what's the solution? Firstly let me tell you a secret, initiate romance in your marriage. If your husband is not romantic or doesn't do anything starting with an 'R,' don't get frustrated or angry because this will just make things worse. Just take the onus of making the relationship more romantic on your own shoulders. Secondly, remember that communication is very important if you want to make your marriage a romantic one. Please understand that he is not a magician who can understand your thoughts automatically. You have to speak up. Men are simple beings. They are not like us. They are less innovative and better at following what others tell them to do when it comes to matters pertaining to the heart. So lead him on.

Most of the women just keep complaining that their husbands are not romantic. Still, the question is, even if we suppose you are the only romantic one in your relationship, what are you doing to express it? Are you preparing a candlelight dinner for him often? Are you buying romantic gifts for him? Are you decorating your home in a special way for the anniversary? Are you booking a vacation for you both to spend some time together? If the answer to the above questions is yes, then don't worry be patient, the day will come soon when he too will learn by watching you and sweetheart if the answer to the above question is 'no,' then make a start to turn on the romance in the relationship merely blaming it all on the husband isn't going to change things.

The point here is that the biggest thing which we as married women yearn for is a bit of romance because we women might be given the best of diamonds as a gift. Still, nothing replaces a little bit of romance. Still, in India, marriage is not a union between two individuals but two families. Though this line is stale, we know how real it is. In our Indian society, romance comes after all the other responsibilities which we have towards our family. It should be accumulated in that little leftover time that we get after fulfilling all the never-ending demands of our family members, which means romance is not considered important. Apart from some modern Indian families, no effort is made to give the young or old couple a little bit of time for themselves. Whereas in western culture, a husband and wife don't feel guilty to call a nanny to babysit their children so that they can go and have a dinner date or spend some time alone.

In India, our children are such an integral part of our marriage that we don't leave them for a single moment to enjoy ourselves. If the grandparents are there, you might be lucky to sneak now and then for a movie or dinner (if your child is not pulling down the heaven with his screams), but if you live alone with your children, bye-bye romance and welcome parenthood. I have heard every other woman complaining that their romantic life has ended (imagine the lives of those who had kids after a year of getting married) but ask these women why. They say kids don't give them any alone time. I sometimes ask the question the other way round, do you give your kids time? I mean, we are so much influenced by how our parents brought us up that we are doing the same things with our children, but the truth is our children are not us.

The way we connected with our parents, our kids don't with us. Our kids have a life of their own pretty early on because of the advent of social media. They might be sitting right before our eyes, but they are mentally living with their friends. Nowadays, kids are far smarter and more independent than we were. Still, we don't stop spoon-feeding our kids and keep pulling them towards ourselves and our marriage. Rather than let both things grow separately in a healthy manner, we make a cocktail of our marriage and parenting. I am not suggesting that you ignore your kids, but a healthy balance must be maintained between the two regarding your marriage and kids. Sometimes we women ourselves are murderers of our romance life.

I have a friend who is not ready to let her daughter sleep in a separate room as she fears the child might be scared to sleep alone, but to realize when the child is not a child is a huge task at hand. Her daughter is fourteen years, and still, she sleeps in her parent's bed. It's not that they don't have a separate room, but still, the girl is treated as a child. I mean, in such a relationship where the children are always hovering around you, imagine the level of romance in the couple's marriage. Her husband tried to reason it out with her, but she was too adamant and clingy to let the girl sleep alone. This type of clingy behaviour is neither good for your marriage nor for your child's proper development. Your marriage is an example of how your kids will view and conduct their own married life, so you should make it a point to set a good example. Your kids must understand that you and your partner are a couple and need some private time. Setting this demarcation is very important if you want to live your life romantically as a couple and not just as a parent, which most of us do.

To keep the romance alive in your marriage, it's important to first consider yourself as a man and wife. All the rest of the relationship tags as a mom, dad, daughter-in-law, aunt, and this. That should follow your primary relationship and not vice versa. You should make it a point to celebrate your special days romantically innovatively. You should listen to music, dance spontaneously, go for long drives, short trips and should stop being serious all the time just because you have become parents or have reached a certain age. You should never ever stop feeling young from within. You must also remember that romance doesn't start with flowers and ends with dinners. Cooking your husband's favorite dish is also romance, and so is surprising him with a hug now and then. Romance is that little flutter in your heart which you feel when you see your husband or the joy which shows on your face when he returns home after work and trusts me if you don't let this , feeling die and keep it alive, your husband will feel it too, and all this is possible by one magic trick which I told you keep your partner at the top of the list of all relationships and watch the magic happen.

CHAPTER IV

Attention Please

It is strange that when couples were living in a joint family system, there were fewer divorces. Now, when couples are living in a nuclear family, the divorce rate has increased manifoldly. Aren't the couples living alone without any family interference supposed to live a more happy life? It seems the answer is a 'No' if we go by the figures. Surprisingly, the couples living in a large family are more connected with each other whereas generally, we are under the impression that the couples living with the family are hardly into each other as they don't get much alone time to spend or they are always busy in fulfilling the responsibilities of the family. However, sometimes appearances are deceptive. I have a friend named *Shweta* who lives in a big family with her in-laws, two brothers-in-law, Sisters-in-law, their children.

All in all, around fifteen members are there in her family. When I asked her one day about how does she manage her marital life with so many people around, she laughed and told me it's very easy. It's not as it looks like. She told me various things like having to do less work as all the women of the house share the chores, the parties and weddings they attend due to a large number of relatives, the fun they have with children, and so on. However, one thing which she mentioned really struck a chord with me. She told me that her marriage is still fresh because of living in a joint family. She told me that since they have limited alone time during the day, there is always a sort of attraction and longing to be with each other in them. They look forward to the time of the day when they can retire to their bedroom and discuss things or when they leave their children home to enjoy a dinner date. She said since there are so many outings and parties and so many people in their lives, they always have something or someone to discuss. It's like "sharing a secret with your confidante," she said blushingly.

After my conversation with her, my entire opinion about the joint family system changed, and I thought that she may be right up to a large extent. The couples who live alone hardly have topics to talk about as mostly it happens that this nuclear couple has fewer social invitations or whatever invitations they get are generally from their friends who too are mostly like them. When a couple lives alone, they have so much time with each other that spending alone time hardly excites them. Even when they have alone time, there is hardly something to discuss, especially if they are still without kids. This type of couple is mostly in a job, and a major part of their day is spent at the office. Life for them becomes a bit boring after the initial honeymoon phase is over. It's like they are together but not attentive to each other.

I may not pinpoint the multiple factors responsible for this change in marital relationships, but one thing which kills the marriage for sure is 'Attention.' Just like a plant needs an adequate amount of water to survive, neither less nor more. Similarly, a couple should give sufficient active attention to each other and make the other person feel special. It doesn't matter whether you are living in a joint family or a nuclear one.

When I was in college, I read a poem by Robert Browning 'My Last Duchess.' This poem was written in 1842, nearly 200 years ago, and the context holds true even today. Browning depicts a Duke in this poem who gets his

Duchess killed because he thinks that the Duchess doesn't give him special attention and treats him just like all the other people in the palace. Honestly speaking, the theme of this poem always confused me, and I always thought that maybe the Duke was a cruel, mad person who killed his wife for nothing. I was never able to grasp what the Duke wanted from his wife? The wife was good to all she met, but she was good to him too. So what would have driven the Duke to kill her?

Years have passed since I have read this poem, but the poem's theme pops up in my mind every time I see a person struggling for the undivided attention of their spouse or when I witness a marriage dying a slow death due to a shortage of attention. So what do we mean by attention? You think that attention is to take care of all the small needs of your husband, of the house, kids, finances, his parents, relatives, friends, what else is left now? Here is where you falter, darling; you can't give your husband the same amount of attention as you give to all your other responsibilities and relatives. You have to give him more time and special attention. However, the truth is we women do the opposite. We give the least amount of our attention to him and maximum to others, and this is where the problems in our marriage start cropping up because of the lesser the attention, lesser the communication and lesser the communication lesser the understanding and lesser the understanding, lesser the bond and lesser the bond lesser the closeness and lesser the closeness more the chances to fall apart.

Men are like kids, just like our kids want our attention all the time when they are young same is true about our husbands. The only difference is our kids grow up and stop craving our attention, but our husband's demand for our attention keeps growing with age. They always want to be the center of our world. They don't like it if we replace them with anyone else. You must have heard about men who are jealous of their kids because they think the kids are contenders of their wives' attention. Some men openly complain about this change and are not happy about the fact that their wives are devoting their time and attention to the kids solely. Men want our undivided attention. They want us to listen only to them when they are talking. They want us to be attentive to them when they are complaining to us. They want us to remember their preferences and dislikes. They want us to compliment them when they dress up or get a new haircut. They will be reluctant to share their office problems with us, but if we make an effort and show interest in their work, they will be more than happy to talk their hearts out with us. In short, they are not much different than us.

However, the only difference we should understand here is that we women by nature develop a close bonding with many people in our lives, whether it's our friends, parents, or kids but our husbands just have us to rely upon when it comes to such bonding. They can't rely on all they meet because of maybe their nature or maybe because they spend most of their lives in a professional world surrounded by colleagues and bosses. We are their only go-to when it comes to all things emotional.

We must understand this and give them our time and undivided attention. We must be interested in what they like and learn about those things or maybe learn about them. Even though sometimes we may not fully understand the technical mumbo jumbo and their fascination with cars and gadgets or their office problems, we must make a sincere effort to understand them. Only this can make us connect with them truly. If we fail to do so, then men generally start leading a lonely life or start depending upon their friends and sometimes start finding solace in extramarital affairs. So ladies, pay attention.

Now some women fail to understand this need of their husbands by a mile. Nowadays, mostly with Whatsapp, Facebook, Instagram, some women have started spending their time on social media a lot. They keep talking to their friends over the phone or updating their statuses and making videos and vlogs and whatnot. It doesn't matter to them whether the husband is around or not. They keep themselves busy with the phone always, and if they are not on the phone the rest of the time, they are always too busy with their household chores or their kids or their friends or their jobs. Their husbands come as the last priority for them. It's not that they don't give time to their husbands or don't talk to them, but there are hardly any qualitative, connective talks. Their conversations can be labeled as routine affairs, not a 'soul connect' type.

These poor women can feel it and sometimes know that they don't have that type of deep connection with their spouses, but they fail to understand where they are going wrong. So the first golden rule for such women is 'no phone when husband is around.' Discard your phone till your husband is at home. You may do all that you want, but in his absence, because I have heard many a husband complaining that their wives are always on the phone. Stop and think, is it really worth it. Something that is affecting your relationship with your husband to such an extent that you are losing connection with him can't be good. Isn't it?.

You must give 'special attention,' attention mixed with interest to your husband and the things which he likes. This deep, sincere attention is what is required to make your relationship great with your husband. To develop a friendship beyond just the mere relationship of husband and wife. Remember, your husband is the most important person in your life. No matter what is your relationship with others, your parents, your kids, your friends but it is he who is going to be there for you till the end, and it is he who is for you in the present too, so never neglect your husband try to build a beautiful relationship with him rather than a routine relationship with him. Remember, attention begets attention.

CHAPTER V

Wake Up! You Are Being Hurt

From an early age, I have had a flair for languages. Growing up in a multilingual society, I picked up many languages naturally, and my inclination towards the etymology of languages drove me further to take classes in European languages. The melancholy is that you tend to forget most of the language once you leave these classes if you are not using them often. However, I was enrolled in one such class when I got engaged. I was super excited to share the news with my friends and did so happily in my language class. Now there was one middle-aged European lady in her 40s who used to be my classmate. I remember she was very good at cooking and would often bake cakes and bring them to the class. She was a very practical and strong type of lady.

However, when I shared the news of my engagement with her, she congratulated me and, after a moment, said to me in her heavily accented Dutch English, "Jeet always remember, the first slap should be the last slap." I was totally taken aback by her comment. I was like, what a weird lady to comment like this while I am sharing the best news of my life with her. However, she continued speaking to me and added that "if you keep quiet and don't take action against the first slap, it is going to bring in many more, and the violence will aggravate. So if things come to such a passé, either hit back or make sure that the first slap is the last slap'".

At that time, I didn't know what she was saying and why she had to make such a comment. But somehow, her advice always adhered to me. By God's grace in my marriage, things never came to that first slap ever, but down the line, as a married woman, I have witnessed many women silently suffering physical violence. In fact, the woman who gave me the advice was herself married two times. Her comment made me think that maybe she was a victim of domestic violence in her first marriage, which made her walk out of it. So if you are a victim, remember, 'first slap is the last slap.' You can fight back. You can warn the other person that you will call it quits and then stick to your ultimatum if this happens again. You can involve your family, shame him by mentioning it in the common friend circle and do something that makes him realize his mistake. Don't feel ashamed of opening up about it, as no matter what, a man can never have the right to hit you.

However, it's easy to fight physical abuse, but what about psychological abuse. In modern-day society, men are not crude enough to beat their wives, which was very common in the 80s and 90s. Thanks to Sharukh Khan and his directors who introduced the 'hero' who was not only a macho figure but a man who respected his women and had a friendly relationship with her. I truly believe that cinema affects our society a lot, and every male tries to copy the hero shown on the celluloid screen, consciously or subconsciously. I mean, if you watch the 70s and 80s movies, the hero would slap the heroine if she spoke back or did something which didn't fall in line with the hero's expectations, and consequently, slapping a woman was not a big thing up to 1980 s 1990s in the society too.

However, this visible abuse has been replaced by a more subtle abuse by many men nowadays. They are too conscious about their image. Women are more strong and financially independent, and they know that women are not solely dependent on them. However, the basic desire to dominate a woman is latent in every man. They can't just accept that women can be better than them though deep down, every man knows that women are far better than them in every field and have been endowed with multi-tasking abilities and more patience, tolerance, and emotional strength.

You are constantly being reminded about your duties and responsibilities as if you are a child. Most Indian men have this awful habit of judging their household chores as a routine affair. I have seen some women washing a white shirt three to four times because their husbands like it spick and span. It reminds me of a weird and funny incident that I witnessed as a child. Those were the days when neighbors were like an extended family, and people will know about each other's family members just like their own family. Privacy, disturbance, me time, these types of notions didn't exist at that time, and people were more open. Most of our winter afternoons were spent on the terrace where all the other aunties would also come to lie down under the sun and chit-chat about their lives. Those sun-soaked winter afternoons are some of the most cherished memories of my childhood. It happened on one such afternoon that when Reema aunty came to spend her afternoon on the terrace. She noticed that her husband's white shirt, which she had put on to dry, had caught color from the other clothes. She became too tense. Her face was petrified, and her body started shaking on seeing the shirt in such a condition. The other women noticed it and understood the situation in moments.

It was an open secret that her husband was a very particular kind of man when it came to his clothes, and he liked his dresses to be immaculate. He fussed a lot about his clothes and would spend hours ironing his pants, not even trusting the laundry man to do it properly. He would walk slowly to the office in the morning, fearing that he might destroy the crease of his pants. Needless to say, a colour stain on the white shirt of such a man would be enough to drive him furious. So to mellow down the wrath of the man-god, all the women teamed up to eradicate the stain, and we kids were their assistants. One aunty told us to go and fetch baking soda from her house, another instructed us to go and bring the bleach, someone suggested to go and bring salt, and someone suggested to go and bring soapnut water. We all ran towards our targeted units, and in no time, all the stain freeing items in the world were lying in Front of the aunties. The stained shirt was our enemy, and we all were going to win over the stain.

We kids were excited to see what would happen next. Totally oblivious to the fact that how deep and big the war was. Anyways all the available techniques were used, but the stain didn't go away completely. In fact, the affected area got a bit discoloured, and the shirt looked two shades of white. All the aunties felt defeated and sad, and as if the sun had also accepted the defeat, it started to set. The aunties were unhappy and started comforting Reema aunty, who was in trouble. At this very moment, I don't know what happened. Reema aunty got up, took the shirt, and hurled it from the terrace like a ball. Some aunties shouted to stop the shirt from falling as if the shirt would listen to their voice and obey, some screamed, and we children flocked to the parapet to witness the fate of the shirt. The white shirt was flying freely like a dove as if it was tired after the experiments which were carried out on it. Eventually, the shirt landed on the roof of another house. All the ladies gathered on the parapet and asked Reema aunty about what she had done and why? Reema aunty just smiled and replied, "now it is stained beyond cleaning," and all the aunties broke out in laughter.

We were made to swear by all the women that this should remain a secret and should never come out. I think I broke the promise after 30 years, but I think it's ok to do so now. I often remember that incident and think about that shirt episode. In my heart of hearts, I admire Reema Aunty and think how easily she converted the whole situation from a tense one to a humourous one. I also often remember the camaraderie those women shared and their laughter after the debacle. Every time it brings a smile to my face, and that floating white shirt seems like the spirit of women who, no matter what, will always fly free.

However, if we study the situation closely, we will see a pattern of abuse in it. What is abuse? According to me, anything that is forced upon you and adds stress and sadness to you is abuse. As I write this chapter, I don't know how many women in the world are facing such abuse in their marriages. Some husbands keep adding to their wives' stress. Starting from the first cup of tea to the last meal of the day. These husbands think that it is their moral right to comment on each and every work done by their wives. The tea is not boiled properly, the sugar is more or less, and the milk is not adequate. Some of them are such idiots that they can comment on the tea made and served temperature. The breakfast, lunch, dinner, snacks all meet the same fate. The poor wives are always stressed to lay down the perfect meal in front of the ever-complaining husbands.

However, the same husband has no problem bringing guests to dinner parties, sometimes announcing that the guests will be coming over for dinner at the last hour. At those dinner parties, he will forget to find faults with the food and deem it fit to be served to the guests. Imagine it, being scrutinized throughout your life for something you do daily, isn't this abuse?. Besides the clothes and food, the Indian husbands keep commenting on the cleanliness maintained in the house, children's study, children's behaviour, wife's appearance, wife's relatives, and every other topic which may come under their preview. They think themselves to be smarter than their wives as if by birth right. Always criticizing, never appreciating, and why is that because they don't do the same work themselves? Hence it's too easy to criticize.

There is also another breed of abusers.From day one of the marriage, they will try techniques to demean the wife by blaming everything wrong in the marriage on the wife. They will make the wife believe that she is the one who is always at fault and is a fight-mongering devil. For example, suppose the wife reminds the husband to pay the electricity bill on the breakfast table. In that case, he will blame that she is out to ruin her day by reminding her as he has an important meeting in the office that day. Suppose the wife asks him to attend a particular function. In that case, he will get irked first as to why do they need to go there in the first place. If he agrees, he will make it a point to make the wife wait and behave as if he has done a huge favour by agreeing to attend that function.On the contrary, if he wants the wife to attend some function, he will behave as if he has done a favour by asking her to come along.

You might think I am speaking about some timid housewife ruled by the cruel husband, no darling, I am talking about the smartest of us, women working as bank officers, teachers, government officers, ask anyone and they will tell you that they are going through this. In fact,

80% of women of all categories face this kind of mental torture. There are many husbands nowadays who abuse their wives in such a manner that even the wives are not aware of the abuse, but they are in constant stress and are unhappy in their respective marriages. This type of abuse is taking place mostly in educated and well-off families. Especially where the wife is smart, educated, and comes from an equally well-off family. Why do some men behave in such a manner? The answer is the same, to dominate the women and feel themselves superior satiating their male egos simultaneously.

Why is it that the husband has to be in the role of some kind of an authoritative figure? Why does a wife's life have to be a journey or a job to constantly please the husband? Why can't the husband and wife live together as equals and friends? These are some questions that are to be answered by both men and women alike. I know some men who feel really guilty after behaving in such a manner with their wives but can't just seem to control this urge to prove their superiority.On the contrary, I know women who have taken divorces and are living a single life but who have never confronted their husbands about their behaviour or have tried to communicate about their distress. The truth is, as I said earlier, our feelings are a dangerous thing. We feel certain things, but we don't know from where those feelings have originated and when.

If women can recognize this silent abuse, they will address it sooner, and maybe it can save many homes and lives. Similarly, men must also keep themselves in the women's shoes and think about the repercussions their day-to-day actions have on the women. Abuse is a double-edged weapon that harms both parties until someone is a psycho or sadist. Hence, we must be aware of the abuse and try to do away with it to live a more happy and healthy life.

CHAPTER VI

Mouth, Heart and Ears

Remember those days when you and your husband chatted for hours on the phone before marriage. Those golden days when it seemed your talks wouldn't ever end, and you imagined what it would be like when you both would stay together under the same roof. You imagined those dinners where both of you will just go on and on, chatting over topics that both of you are so passionate about. You thanked God that you had found someone with whom you could talk your heart out, and you started believing seriously that you were lucky to get a guy like your husband, who is such a great communicator.

Fast forward five years ahead, both of you have been sitting beside each other on the same sofa for the last five hours and have not spoken a single word to each other. Highlights of your conversation are enquiring about what would the other person like to eat or watch on the TV. Both of you are happily immersed in your respective phones when you go out for dinners, and you don't find a single topic under the sun to discuss with each other. You wonder what went wrong? Where is that efficient communicator whom you married? How do things come to such a passé? When did both of you become just like any other couple sitting next to you in the restaurant? You keep asking yourself and fail to get an answer, and then you find solace in the exact same complaints of your friends and close the chapter, thinking it happens with everyone after marriage. Burying all the ideal dreams about your marriage. Once this initial acceptance takes place, both of you fall into a routine of non-conversation and gradually start drifting apart mentally and emotionally because the connection is gone

So what went wrong? The first thing which is quite obvious is that the newness and curiosity about each other fade away once we start living together. We know everything about each other, the families, the relatives, the friends, the highs and the lows, and there is nothing left to talk about. Whereas before marriage, we take pleasure in imagining what type of room our spouse would be living in now, we are not even concerned about his new office cabin. As we live together, the most vital element that keeps the interest alive is 'curiosity,' which goes away, and 'i know ' sets in. The second and most important thing that affects our communication is our expressions and gender differences. When we talk over the phone, we can't see the other person's instant reactions to our words, so we just keep talking our heart out, and the other person, if he doesn't like what we are saying, changes the subject or leaves the topic midway to avoid confrontation as he is also well aware of the newly formed relationship and values the relationship more than the topic of discussion.

However, when we talk face to face, we can gauze the reaction of the other individual instantly, and hence many times, we avoid talking or don't feel comfortable talking about something which seems to irk our partner. This is the first glitch in communication between the husband and wife. Besides this, since the relationship is established now, both the partners start to assert their opinions more aggressively rather than avoid the topic. They find out that they don't have the same opinion about many a thing. Hence, they either start influencing the other person to accept their point of view or if the discussion starts converting into quarrels, they start avoiding talking on the topic altogether. Slowly and steadily, this list of 'not to be discussed' topics piles up so much so that every other topic to be discussed with each other seems like an invitation to quarrel. The result is a deadly silence. However, trust me, if this 'not to be discussed' list keeps increasing, soon your marriage will be in the doldrums.

Besides this, there is a marked difference in the communication patterns of men and women, which I prefer to call 'gender difference' in communication. The women mostly have the habit of speaking about the same topic multiple times, and we never come straight to the point. For example, if we face a certain problem, we talk about it to all our friends and family. It doesn't matter if we have ten friends and have to narrate the same incident ten times over. We keep repeating ourselves. In the process, we forget about our husband or other family members who have to listen to the whole conversation ten times over. Many of my friends tell me that their husbands or children just don't listen to them at all. They are surprised that though they say the same thing three or four times, the family members act as if they haven't heard a single word of what they have been saying.

Do you wonder why? The reason is that your voice has become the background music to them, constantly playing and repeating itself. They are confident that the repeat version will be available shortly, even if they miss what you say. This negligent attitude has developed because of your own behaviour. We women speak our hearts out and don't care much about the words we use. Our main focus is on the information to be imparted rather than how it is imparted. With men, it's the opposite. They don't like to talk about the same thing constantly. Men have a more solution-finding type of brain rather than problem discussion kind of brain. So if you are facing a similar situation, stop acting in the same manner. Let your speech hold some value for them. If possible, don't repeat yourself.

However, sometimes the problem is not of communicating but of 'what' to communicate. Have you thought that why do your communication flow with your friends and your chats last for hours with them whereas? The same is not true about your conversations with your husband. Now there are two reasons here, and firstly, some men are very hot-tempered and quarrelsome by nature. Talking to them is fighting. These kinds of men are too smart for their own good. The moment their wives open their mouths, they start speculating what she is going to say next. They are too impatient to hear them out and always cut them short, and hence the conversation with such a person is curtailed.

I have noticed women living with men and avoiding talking to them from either the fear of making them angry or they just don't find it fulfilling to talk with such a man who dominates the entire conversation. In these types of cases, it doesn't matter 'what' you talk about. Everything leads to a fight. So if you are living with such a man, I would suggest you either maintain distance or make him understand that it won't work like that and if it doesn't work then either live with it or run out of it, it's your decision. The second reason you seem tongue-tied when it comes to talking with your husband is that time changes everything. The interests we have before marriage or in our 30s undergo a major shift once we are in our 40s. Priorities shift, ambitions shift, and opinions change, and you must try to keep up with the changing personality of your spouse.

Just talking about the kids and relatives is not enough. You have to look a bit into your husband's brains. What excites him, what are his favourite topics, what is going on in his professional life, and so on. If need be eavesdrop a bit on him when he is talking on the phone with his friends, and you will definitely come up with a minimum of five interests which he is passionate about and though it's not necessary that his interests would excite you too(it won't, I know) but you have to get yourself interested in his world to become a part of it.

Mind it, the majority of husbands aren't talkers. If you want to have communication, you have to start talking first, maybe about his colleagues, office problems, or business. He may be reluctant initially, but when he notices that you are genuinely interested, he will start opening up bit by bit. Remember, communication is the key to friendship, and if you can't communicate with your husband, it will be very difficult for you to have a happy and healthy marital relationship. Now the best kind of communication is where a person speaks their mind without any fear. So you have to bring your relationship to such a level of honesty and friendship where both of you can listen to each other without the fear of being judged or reprimanded. If these conditions fall in place, trust me, there is no better friend than your life partner to have the most interesting conversations.

Another big block in a couple's communication is time. You may have experienced it yourself or have heard your friends complaining that they don't have time to talk. Morning time is full of huff and puff to cook the 'dabbas,' to get the kids ready, and handle the maids. During afternoons the husbands are in office and wives at home. Come evening (if 9PM or 10PM counts as evening), you are busy with dinner and watching television. Whatever little time is spared, you devote it to the kids. So when can you talk? I know a couple who will go for a long drive after dinner for a simple reason because they lived in a joint family, and everyone was always around. I know they solved the biggest of their fights in the car. The drive also took them away from the television and social media, which is the biggest distraction for talking.

So here is an idea, skip that television show and go for a drive. I also know a couple who used to talk a lot in the mornings. My friend has kept a chair in the kitchen itself, and every morning while she was making the tiffin for the husband, her husband would come and sit in the kitchen and have his morning tea and breakfast there only. It was a daily routine with them, and it kept the communication alive. You can also ask your husband to take advantage of the monthly short leaves provided by all the organizations, and you can make the most of it by talking it out.

I had a colleague once who was late at least three times a month. When I asked him how come he was so late to reach at 11 AM in the office he smiled and replied: "I know my half day's salary is deducted if I am even five minutes late then why not work half day if I am late. " I was totally taken aback with his logic as contrary to him I would rush out of my house when I was getting late and many a time my half day's salary had been deducted for reaching five minutes late in the office. Bravo! to the smart employee.

Besides this, you can sometimes order food from outside or go out for dinner to spend some quality time with your better half. Another great way to communicate is WhatsApp. You may chat your heart out to your partner every now and then via this medium. In fact, if you are having a fight, chatting on WhatsApp is a great way to end the fight and make the other person see your point of view as when we are fighting, we mostly focus on the other person's reaction and try even more aggressively to make him see our point of view. Hence the fight is generally useless without any long-term change, but if you talk it out on WhatsApp, it provides you with more peace and clear thoughts to see the other person's opinion and explain yours leading to a more amicable settlement. You can also fix a 'no television time' once a week where the whole family sits and talk, or at least you both sit and talk. So next time, if you feel you don't have time, you may try one of these ideas.

Some women are depressed due to a lack of communication with their husbands. They tell me they have tried everything under the sun to have a heart-to-heart talk with their husbands, but they have failed miserably. As we discussed, men can never understand or talk to us how we want them to. So what can be done? Go to women! I mean, make some good friends or share your thoughts with your girlfriends. A woman only can listen and understand another woman patiently. Besides, we also have the same interests like shopping, clothes, jewelry, etc. Only two women can discuss the different shades of lipsticks or the height of heels. Don't expect it from your husband. However, remember never let out too intimate details of your relationship, even to the best of your friends. In this world, there is no shortage of people who may turn against you at any time. So hold your deepest secrets close to your heart.

As your husband is the most important person in your life, backbiting on him will not only demean your image but may also put you in trouble later. Before divulging any intimate details about your marriage, make sure that the other person is also sharing the same sort of details with you or not. Everyone is not genuine, and eavesdropping is the favorite game of women mostly. So be a good judge of character before indulging in heart-to-heart talks, even with your girlfriends. Remember, your heart should know what your mouth talks, and your ears should hear what the others say.

Never Say Goodbye

It was a winter night and at around 1 AM, we were woken up by loud noises of quarrels and crockery breaking. Our first thought was that some thief had broken into some house, and perhaps a lady was struggling to save her life. We at once came out in our courtyard and started searching for the origin of the noise. We noticed that some other neighbors had also woken up and were loitering around in their balconies and gardens when we came out. As all the adjacent bungalows had low fence walls, we could see each other. I noticed no one was shouting or was trying to run towards the place of action, and in my half-drowsy state of sleep, I wondered why. The noise didn't stop coming, and I heard a woman's scream this time.

My heart sank, and it was then that I noticed that the noise was coming from the house which was just opposite to ours. It was Mrs. Rana's house. She was an old widowed lady who used to live alone. She had one daughter named Anita, who was married and stayed in another town. Anita used to visit her mom quite often as the town where she lived was just a couple of hours away. It didn't take me much time to figure out what was going on. Anita's husband had come along with her, and he was brutally beating Anita in the middle of the night. Since it was a very tough decision to interfere in someone's private matter, we, along with our neighbors, kept standing in our driveway listening to Anita's screams and Mrs. Rana's pleas. My heart sank with each scream of Anita, and I could just imagine the pain she would be feeling.

I felt this strong urge to barge into Mrs. Rana's house and slap Anita's husband for his cruel behavior. But trust me, friend, it's very difficult to take action like this in real life than thinking that one must go and interfere. The quarrel and fight went on for some time, and everything went silent after that. The whole society has witnessed what has happened, many of us were agitated, but all went inside after everything settled. The next morning, I noticed that Anita's car was not there and thought that maybe her husband had left angrily. However, I realized that Anita had gone back to her husband's place in the early morning. I couldn't just believe that a woman could go back to live with such a person who dared to beat her so brutally that too in her mother's house. I shivered, thinking about what sort of treatment Anita would be getting in her in-law's house.

Around one year passed, and things went back to normal. All of us forgot the incident as an out-of-the-blue incident that took place between Anita and her husband. Mrs. Rana looked happy as before, and Anita did visit her sometimes in the last year. It seemed like everything was well in paradise. However, one day Anita came back to her mom's house with big suitcases and some other stuff, and I knew that she had come back forever. Frankly speaking, I felt relieved and happy for the girl. Even while writing this episode, I can recall that chilly winter night and her screams, and still, my heart sinks thinking about it. I struggled to understand how Anita lived with that 'Paan Masala' eating violent pig called her husband. The divorce took place eventually, and Anita started staying along with her mom. The entire neighborhood seemed to be happy for Anita as all of us had witnessed her horrific marriage.

However, I noticed that after some months, the ladies of our neighborhood started match-fixing for Anita. During our common kitty parties or festive occasions, women will start the discussion of Anita's remarriage. Anita would go quiet or sometimes make an excuse to run an errand to avoid such moments, but Mrs. Rana was always made to listen to the benefits of remarrying her daughter. A neighbour even tried to marry her much younger nephew to Anita as all were aware of Anita's good financial inheritance. However, nothing could bring Anita around, and she didn't agree to any of the marriage proposals. She started working for a consultancy, and it seemed that she was happy. Things should have settled amicably for all; however, Anita's rejection of proposals and not conforming to society's rules for women didn't go quite well with the neighbors.

Public memory is very short, and the very same neighborhood, which was sympathetic towards Anita, turned hostile towards her by the end of the second year of her divorce. Everyone very easily forgot about the monster Anita had, and the same old rumors revolving around single divorced women started making the rounds of our neighborhood. Every time I heard someone eavesdropping on her, I felt this rage towards the people who had started blaming Anita for her divorce. How shocking and how shameful it was, but this is the reality of divorce in India. Not only in the case of Anita, but I have witnessed it in many divorce cases that the very people who stand beside the girl during the divorce process turn against them with time. The very own kith and kin start blaming the woman no matter how innocent one is in the entire divorce process. The only thing which seems to go in favour of a divorced woman is remarriage. Imagine the condition of a divorced woman in such circumstances. Surviving a bad marriage then the divorce, which is a mentally, emotionally and financially draining process, doesn't seem to solve the problem completely.

Another very strange phenomenon that I have witnessed in the case of divorce is that the women who still believe in the institution of marriage after coming out of a terrible relationship tend to fall for the same kind of person all over again. Why they choose the same sort of partner is a mystery. If we look into the divorce pattern of countries like the USA, UK, etc., we will come to know that people there marry three or four times only to divorce every time because they tend to marry the same sort of person again and again.

So what's the solution? Should we stay in a marriage even it is like living in hell? Or if the spouse is too abusive, uncaring, and unloving? Should we just stay in a marriage to avoid the problems one faces after divorce? The answer to the above question is that marriage is a far complicated institution rather than just being in love and staying happy with the person. No marriage in the world can vouch for 100% happiness. There are some good days, and then there are days worst than nightmares. Every marriage wants to sacrifice, adjustment and understand. No matter how best a couple we are in our marriage, there is bound to come a time when we feel like leaving each other. Sometimes the fights are circumstantial, and sometimes it seems like every limit has been crossed. But when you think of divorce or running out on the other person, never do it on impulse or on someone else's advice.

Marriage is not just staying with a person, but it stands for your social and financial position, relationships, children, comfort, security, future, old age, and a hundred other complicated emotions. You invest your life, your time, your money, and your soul into your marriage. If you are thinking of divorce, just stop and consider very practically and not just emotionally whether you are ready to give it up. Especially if the other person wants to stay with you and you have more issues with the other person rather than the other way around. I know it's suffocating, it hurts, and it seems that our life is just stuck if we continue like this. But remember, these are our emotions talking if you think with your mind you will get a much more holistic picture. To stay in a marriage is like the tongue staying amongst all those teeth. You may believe whatever you want but the reality is that in our Indian society eventually it's always the Women who get the bad part of the deal. Think very very hard as to why you are divorcing if it's for an illusion of getting someone better or true love, I would suggest check yourself. Grass is not more green on the other pasture always.

Calculate your losses and benefits before proceeding for divorce. Think hard if the problems you are facing in your marriage can be worked out and weigh your problems against the benefits which you are getting from staying in the marriage. If you live happily in your marriage for 300 days and have problems for 65 days, it can be worked upon. Besides this try to evaluate and delve deep about the problems your marriage has and try to fix it. Leaving is always the easiest option and staying is tough but remember tough people last tough situations don't.

CHAPTER VIII

Sex Matters

Why do we get married? Most of us will reply to this question with a platonic answer like we marry so that we may get a companion for life, someone who cares for us, loves us, understands us and blah, blah, blah. Before marriage it seems that it's only that one person (our husband)who is going to cater to all our needs. The concept of a prince on a white horse galloping towards the clouds is an image that every girl sticks to and believes that only he can save her from the atrocities of life. She believes that he will wooosh the magic band on her head, making her happy and complete. However five years on the road to marriage and a girl understands that whatever ideals she wanted to achieve after marriage were all false and misleading.

The real love, care, understanding, companionship doesn't come from one person only. Each need is fulfilled by a different person in our life in a different situation. It's not possible humanly for a single person to cater to all our needs. After marriage our biggest companions are our children and if you are working it's our colleagues. Our mom was, is and always will be our best care taker. Whereas understanding us is concerned it comes a little bit from everyone depending upon their perspective towards us. So if every emotional need of our's is met by someone or the other, why do we get married? The answer is simple, it's sex which makes marriage necessary. No matter how strongly you deny the fact that sex is not all that important for you or you don't need it much or you can do without it. But the truth is that sex is the most important bond which holds the marriage together.

Infact in the first few months especially in arranged marriages, it's sex which sets the tone of marriage and keeps it going. Sex in marriage evolves from playfulness and passion to love and healing in due process gradually. The initial sex in marriage is like an exciting adventure where both the partners are discovering the various facets of the concept of sex but after some years if you are in a healthy marital relationship, sex becomes a sort of reassurance of your relationship, the deep connect, something sacred which you have with one another and don't share with any other person in the world.

However for men sex doesn't change much in concept and they look at it in the same manner as they did it on the first night of the marriage but for a woman sex changes from the nervousness of the first night to emotional bonding of a sound marriage. Women don't view sex as just a physical process, for them it runs deeper and is essential for their physical (speak of the hormones) as well as their mental happiness. Having regular sex boosts a females confidence in her marriage and she feels loved by her partner. Maybe the word love making for sex was invented by a woman. Having sex doesn't only gives a woman a chance to be near to her husband physically but it also reassures her about her position in her husband's life. It's sort of a yardstick with which a woman measures her beauty, her value, her importance and her marriage. Hence to have a healthy sexual relationship is much more important for women than the men.

It should be considered that biologically men and women run on a different sex clock. Whereas men are more charged up before 30 women want it more after 30. Various studies show that women are most sexed up between 30 to 45 years of age rather than their younger and older counterparts. Sadly most of the men develop problems in this department during this age. Presently with the marriage age moving to 27 to 32 years, most of the couples struggle with sexual problems. Whereas we are made to think that it's the males who want all the sex the contrary is true.

I know a girl named Niharika who married at the age of 28 years. She went for an arranged marriage and imagine her shock when she found out on her first night that her husband was having problems in this department. Her husband was very nice and the in-laws family too was immensely loving and caring but this girl felt suffocated. She tried to talk to her husband and told him to get help but he was too much of an indiot to take professional help or do something about it. Her husband like most of the Indian husbands thought that since they are married she will tolerate everything and his love and family comfort will make up for the void which was present in the bedroom.

Niharika came to her mother's house after six months of her marriage and whoever met her, commented on her deteriorated health and dark circles under her eyes. Many a women thought that she was pregnant but the truth was far from it. Surprisingly when she shared her problem with her mother and sister-in-law both panicked and told her to stay mum about it. They tried to make her understand that things will get better and it's just a passing phase in her marriage. It was suggested that she should try to do something, she was given crude tips to handle her sex life. In short as is the practice in our beloved country her husband's problem was totally swept under the carpet and she was made to feel as if it's her fault that things weren't hot and happening between them. Niharika was more disturbed than ever and she started blaming herself for the problem. Before confiding in her family members things were simpler for her. She knew what the problem was and it was not she who was in any way responsible for her husband's physical condition. But after she confided the women of her house made her believe that if her husband isn't feeling sexed up, somehow it's her fault. It's she who couldn't arouse his feelings. She went back to her in-laws family with more suffocation, guilt and self doubt. She started thinking that maybe her mother and sister-in-law are correct, maybe she wasn't that beautiful or maybe she wasn't exciting enough and this 'maybe' costed her a lot for her entire life.

All limits were crossed when one day her mother kept a religious ceremony to pray for Niharika's fertility. I just could not believe my ears when her mother came to invite me for the same. I knew it wasn't Niharika's fault that she wasn't able to conceive and I knew that her mother knew the facts but it seemed that her mother has conviniently forgotten this little detail about the son-in-law. How can she being a mother do this to her daughter? Why wasn't Niharika walking out of the fake marriage? Why was she taking all the blames and sacrificing her life for people who just didn't care for her?

All these questions will always remain unanswered for me as after the initial period of her marriage Niharika has stopped talking about her life with me. I have advised her at that time that she should immediately leave the marriage as six months have already passed and when six months have passed without any initiative from her husband or her husband making an effort to make things right six years will pass too in the same manner. You don't have to eat the entire dish to tell it's taste. However, I think Nikarika has adjusted like thousands of Indian girls who are not able to leave a sexless marriage sometimes due to parental pressure, sometimes due to society and sometimes due to simply acknowledging the fact that sex is the core of marriage. But when do good Indian girls talk about sex or demand it. Sex is a bad thing, '*gandi cheez*' is what we are taught from childhood. Indian girls wait for it till marriage and imagine if you end up like Niharika in a sexless marriage which is very common these days due to effect of modern lifestyle, what happens to your desires.

So what should you do if you are in a sexless marriage?'Run' or 'Fight' just don't give up and let your husband think that you are happy without sex when in reality you are not. You know you are suffering and you 'should' make a big deal about it. Remember if you don't bring it to the forth, your husband will never ever talk about it. As a woman you will suffer more because sex is not only about gratifying your needs but also bringing the next generation into this world and the onus of it lies on a woman primarily. When a woman is not able to conceive everyone thinks that the problem is with the woman. No one thinks that the man can be at fault too. It is you who will be pointed fingers at not your husband such is the way of our society. if you have children and are living in a sexless marriage, still it doesn't make any sense to stay in an unhappy marriage because nowadays the children are very smart and they will know about the hoax of your marriage sooner or later.

They will realize about your unhappiness before you can describe it to them. Besides it's difficult to raise happy children in a house where marriage is another name for stress for both the partners. Sexual dissatisfaction is bound to cause fights between the partners on small pretexts. Though the fights may look unnecessary or illogical to a third person but the core of it is well known to the couple and understood by the children.

It happens with many males that their sexual incompetency make them even more cruel towards the woman. They feel guilty and try to cover it up by finding faults with their wife or instigating fights so that the intimacy level is never reached and they are not reminded about their shortcoming. Many men also try to be even more macho then they really are when they are lacking in bed. But remember don't keep quite, talk about it to your husband even if he is reluctant to get help for his problem tell him that it's not just about him you are also affected by this equally. If he picks up unnecessary fights and stages dramas out of nowhere, look at it from a different point of view and avoid him as much as possible. Don't get entangled in his games and loose your peace because of the fact that he is not strong enough to acknowledge his problem. You are entitled to happiness, never be in self doubt or underestimate yourself. Fight for your conjugal rights and happiness. Sometimes it's just a small problem which could be solved by visiting a doctor once maybe and due to that one delayed visit to the doctor, the relationship between a husband and wife sufffer for years.

Now there are some men and women who use sex as a weaponThey use it as a carrot and stick philosophy and manipulate their partners using this strategy very effectively. I have a friend who has a phrase for settling scores with her husband "bed mein dekh lenge" (will teach him a lesson in bed)and she also advices every other woman facing problem with her husband to do the same. We always laugh when she says this and it has become a sort of joke amongst us. But sometimes I think is it correct to deprive your partner of pleasure, that too regularly so that you may have a upper hand on him or can make him pay for something wrong he did. In this scenario doesn't the husband understands what the wife is upto? Obviously he does and what if one fine day he stops giving in for such tactics. What if gets tired of such tactics and starts looking elsewhere to fend his needs?.

A marriage revolves around sex and intimacy and if that is also not pure, how pure could be one's relationship with her partner? Moreover if one constantly uses sex as a weapon to defeat his opponent then trust me your marriage is going to be like a warfare. We all know by now that sex is very important for our physical and mental well being hence it is very important that we consider it as something which is pleasure, love and peace. Whenever you or your partner think about sex it should bring a sweet smile on your face and not a cunning smile.

The most important thing which keeps your sex life active is the rule of demand and supply. There should be adequate demand from your husband and you should make it sure that you neither build an easy supply nor make it too difficult to meet his demands. You know why jewels are expensive? The reason is they are not easily available like stones. It is the availability of something which decides it's value. If you make yourself available all the time chances are that your husband might get bored too soon and a day would come when you will be running after him to satisfy your physical needs rather than the other way round. Men are curious creatures and once their curiosity dies their interest goes for a toss. They also seldom value things which they get easily. Hence to keep the man's curiosity alive and your value intact make sure that you learn to say no sometimes.

For a woman it's very important that she takes things a bit slowly. Most of the men like to lead from the front when it comes to sexual matters and sometimes initiation from the woman puts them off. Besides men don't like women who are upfront about sex. However there are exceptions to this too and some men never initiate sex at all from the fear of being rejected by their partner. They would always want the wife to take the first step. What category your husband best fits to should be observed by you very closely and you should plan your moves accordingly. After the initial honeymoon phase is over brain plays an equally important part in our sex lives as our physical attributes. You have to be innovative, creative and intuitive if you want to have a happening sex life even after decades of your marriage.

'It is men who lie about their sex life. They have this habit of boasting about their sexual prowess and power. Men make up things to show how macho they are and what beasts they are in bed. We have often heard the above mentioned statements about men and often come across jokes about a man's lie about his masculine powers but hold on it's not just only men who lie about their sex lives women do it too. Yes, you heard it right. There are many women who lie about their awesome sex lives. How their husband just can't keep his hands off her. How adventurous they are in bedroom or how frequent are their marathon sex sessions and so on. Honey, don't fall in someone's trap. Never compare your sex life with anyone else. It doesn't matter if Mrs so and so is getting it five times a week or Mrs so and so is not getting anything in a year. You and your sex life is your private business. Just like everyone's plate has different quantities of dishes on it, same is true about sexual needs. If you are happy with your sex life then there is no need to be intimidated by others.

I know so many women who keep comparing their sex lives with that of others and keep depressed. Whereas if they just concentrate on their own intimacy levels, they would be surprised to know that they don't need to be unhappy. Moreover if their sexual expectations are not met by their partners then also what good would it bring to compare. Best thing is when you hear someone bragging about their great sex achievements listen to it merely as an entertainment don't take it much seriously or try to delve deep into the private lives of people. Trust me, the more you stay away from the private lives of other people the more peaceful and happy you live your own life. Concentrate on your own sex life and try to make it more happy and satisfying for yourself and your partner. Communicate about your needs openly to your partner and give an ear to their desires too because sex matters matter.

CHAPTER IX

He is your Hero Baby

Do you know why they say that behind every successful man there is a woman? The reason is that it's only a woman who can motivate a man to do much better than he actually can. A woman has the power to make her and her husband's life hell or heaven. The husband can never make a woman's life hell because we women are far more better equipped to deal with our emotions and have a far stronger support system than men to cope with our problems and miseries. To understand this we may look into the lives of our poor maids. We all are aware that six out of ten Indian maids have a good for nothing, alcoholic husband. If you meet these men you will see that these are men who have been defeated by life and who have lost all hope. It's not that they don't realise that they are doing wrong with their families but it's simply that they don't have the fighting spirit to make things right. They may seem to us as stupid alcoholic idiots but deep below their facade they are too egoistic men who want all the respect which a man of a male dominated society looks for sans fulfilling any duty.

They are too smart to know that their socioeconomic condition doesn't help them to get the needed respect hence they try to get it all by beating and dominating their poor wives. On the other hand when you look at our Indian maids no matter what the situation is you will find them smiling always. They feed their children, their husbands and their extended family. They educate their children. They help the other women who are in similar situation and yet they seldom complain and can crack a joke and laugh on the situation. These poor women and men are examples of the coping skills of men and women amongst adverse circumstances and needless to say women come out as winners.

Women are far more better than men whether it's handling disappointments, grief, set backs or emotional turmoil. This is the reason that woman act as a backbone for men. Men need lot of motivation to keep going. They are too impatient and loose hope very fast. It's the women who keep them going by supporting them, motivating them and praising them. A man who gets love, praise and motivation from his wife can move the mountains. However if a man is constantly nagged and insulted by his wife, he looses all interest in bettering himself or his position. Now there is also another category of men, we may label them as 'Kalidasa' men who like the great poet achieve greatness if they are rebuked by their wives. But these Kalidasa men are rare. Most of the men give it up all if they don't feel appreciated by the wife. Remember men have the capacity to be very distant when it comes to emotions.

I have observed couples where the wife is a loud mouth and keeps insulting her husband on one pretext or the other and it seems that men are very patient or are so nice that they keep smiling and never get into a fight with the wife or stop their wives while they are insulting them openly. But trust me this silence of men is lethal. These men do look like henpecked husbands but don't the look of it deceive you. If you probe further you will either meet a man who is not interested to do a single thing for his family or is causing constant torture to his wife by silently doing all those things which makes the wife mad. It's like a cold war. On the face value it seems wife is winning the battle but trust me she has lost it big time.

Husband and wife are like two parts of one body. It's impossible to be happy if any one part of your body is in pain or to ignore it. The more you fight with eachother more unhappy you will be. The more you try to show eachother down, both of you will be looking at the bottom of things. The more you insult your partner chances are more insults will come your way. The best way out is that you should let love and peace prevail. Try to encourage each other to strive for better things. Praise each other. Appreciate each other. Give confidence to eachother. Make the other person feel happy about himself and give faith to the other person that you will have his back no matter what may come. There are many similes which are drawn to explain the relationship of husband and wife and each similie always stresses on the fact that they are equally important in the unit of marriage and this is the unparallel truth.

As a wife it's in your best interest to fight less and motivate more. Never insult your husband even when alone, leave aside Infront of others. Try to give him confidence and praise him for all the little things he does. Motivate him to do better and make him believe that he can. There is nothing in this world which you can't make him do with your love. Stop being a nagging, dismissive, insulting wife, if you are one. Analyze your actions and think hard about the way you behave with him. If he is the one to be blamed for bad behaviour sit with him and explain to him calmly about what he does and how it effects you. You can also inform him that you are going to behave with him in the exact same manner as he does with you for the next fifteen days. There are chances that he will realize his mistakes in the given period.

Always remember he is your hero and you can make him one with your love, intelligence and behaviour. If you will keep a happy and peaceful environment at home chances are there will be more success at his professional front. It's not important to win every fight and argument or reply to him on every silly accusation he makes. Sometimes just letting things go and avoiding fights goes a long way in changing the person rather than trying to show him his mistake everytime. The best part is more peaceful and happy he is the more happy you are. Listen patiently to his future plans and try to adjust if you think that his plans sound good enough. Be ready for change and challenges if he is trying to do it for better prospects.

I have seen women who are not at all comfortable to come out of their comfort zone and in turn they force their husbands to abandon any plans of future development. These woman are biggest bloopers when it comes to their husband's and family's well being. Some women are also such pessimist that they keep refusing everything which the husband tries to suggest for a better future. As a wife you should show confidence in your husband's ability and should support him with positivity and open mindedness. If he wants to try something new you should support him rather than pull him down. You should voice your fears about his decisions but if he is logical enough to settle your fears you should not be adamant to stop him just because you feel so. Suppory him to be successful. The more successful he is the more you enjoy the fruits of his success. It is not for nothing that they say that behind every successful man there is a woman.

CHAPTER X

Happiness is Made

My friend Leena got married around 18 years ago. After Leena's marriage it was just she and her husband living in a small city away from their family. It was a new city with zero friends for her. There wasn't any mall, theater, museum, library, park or any such place where she could go out to spend some time and to top it all, there were electricity cuts for four hours twice a day. The concept of inverters was new and internet was killingly slow if one operated it from the laptop. Moroever at that time only yahoo was available and there was no whtsapp, Instagram or facebook by which one could keep in touch with friends or family. Phone calls and emails were the only saviours.

During the first few months when Leena was trying to figure out her future prospects. She had ample amount of time in her hands. Once her husband left for his office the only thing she had to do was to wait for his return. Since she hardly had any friends or too much of work to do she started getting bored and lonely. Her husband was her only saviour from the boring life in that small town. After he came back from office, they went out for a drive or to eat or to just take a bike ride. Slowly it started happening that Leena had laid the onus of her happiness on her husband. His moods started to have a huge effect on Leena. If he was disturbed she got disturbed too and his cheerfulness cheered her up. If he informed Leena that he was going out to spend some time with his friends in the evening or he is having a boy's night out something will sink inside Leena, as the thought of spending more hours alone without anyone to talk to or do anything or even watch television would terrify her.

She spent the whole day alone but to spend the evenings alone came as an extra burden. Her husband has become a fulcrum of her life. She kept thinking that when he will come he will do this and that for her and they will go out or he will tell her how his day went and so on and so forth. It was like he was the only happiness she had. She started becoming more and more dependent upon him and this didn't change even when she took up a job herself. Somewhere her happiness lied only with her husband now. She didn't want to do anything which led to fun without him. He used to encourage her to go ahead and have fun and many a times he tried to make her understand that it's not necessary for him to be present always, for her to be happy but nothing can make her understand this logic. Leena kept postponing her plans to go for shopping or watch a movie or visit friends as she always wanted to share her every happy moment with her husband. Just being around him made her happy.

Her husband got really frustrated because of her behaviour because he wanted her to be independent and happy. At times there were quarrels amongst them due to this clinginess of Leena. This went on for years and then suddenly one day she had this Eureka moment. It just struck her that why is it that she expects her husband to make her happy why can't it be the other way around. Why doesn't she try to make him happy? Why can't she be happy herself? The moment these questions surfaced, it solved many of her life's problems. she felt less restless and more free.

She was already doing lot of activities but at the back of her mind the feeling to be with her husband was always there. But now she started living in the moment. Besides this she also started creating small surprises for her husband or a gift or a surprise dinner etc so that her husband could feel happy because of her. She observed that with the change in her behaviour her husband started appreciating her more and somewhere he felt more relaxed. This resulted in more happiness and peace amongst them both. She came to a conclusion that no one is responsible for our happiness, we ourselves are responsible for it.

When we are in love sometimes we get so attached to the person that we forget the concept of giving space to the other person altogether. It happens with us unknowingly and we sometimes are in such a love doze state that we fail to analyze whether the other person is feeling good about it or is it causing him suffocation. Many amongst us commit the same mistake as Leena. We women want our husband to share everything with us. Our happiness is sort of incomplete if our better halves are not present beside us. There are many women who wait patiently for the husband to be present, then there are those who fight with the husband to be around and the last category includes of those depressed women who have tried both the above techniques but due to x, y, z reasons, whose husbands aren't able to devote time to them. I really feel pitty for the last category because they are the worst sufferers. The crime however of all the three categories is that they love their husbands too much and have very high expectations out of their relationship. However they forget that sometimes doing something rather than always expecting, can make us more happy. So ladies don't wait for your husband to make you happy try to do it the other way round. Besides learn to enjoy yourself, give importance to other people who are in your life. Don't just concentrate on hubby dear only.

There is another problem in staying happy in a marriage and that is, it doesn't matter what you do but your husband is never happy. He keeps finding fault with everything you do or keep shouting or is always in an irked state of mind. This takes a toll on the woman and she loathes her husband. She wants him to be out of the house always. The moment the husband walks in house the wife feels suffocated. In this situation try to ignore your husband and consider it as the part of his nature. Communicating to him about his bad behaviour and showing him the mirror about his actions and how his actions are causing an unpleasant environment in the home can also help a lot. He will definitely deny the charges against him but you must be strong yet polite. Remember fighting with swords will only lead to more blood shed. The trick is to hide the swords of both the sides.

In marriage it's important to speak out the good, bad, ugly because trust me it's not that both the partners don't know your ugly side or their ugly side but by communicating about it, you both can transform it to beautiful from ugly. However before walking down the lane of harsh truths try to make a more happier environment in your home by being polite and appreciative. You cannot win with a child by arguing. Men sometimes behave very childishly and illogically in these situations try to keep your calm and handle the situation with wit. Appreciate your man and tell him about his good qualities. The more you praise him more happier he will be. Because the biggest desire in this world of every human being is getting appreciated. Your praise will elevate his mood and his confidence whereas your constant nagging and negative comments on him will lead to fights. So try a more positive approach and see how wonderfully it works.

You are not only responsible for your own happiness but also for the happiness of your children and husband. If you keep this small fact at the forefront of your mind you will be more positive. The best part of this idea is that your brain starts working overtime towards creating happiness rather than finding faults or fights. Since you have chosen happiness you start avoiding situations which may lead to ugly confrontations and this in turn will lead to a more peaceful you. Remember we have no control over the various incidents of life or others behaviour towards us but we definitely have our reaction in our hands. Happiness is not something which happens naturally like rain but it is made by our daily actions and reactions. If you are happy everything around you will be happy too as happiness and laughter is contagious.

Another huge reason why most Indian women are unhappy is that they feel they could have done this or that as per their educational qualifications, but they didn't get a chance to do so due to marriage. These women are constantly living in a complex of some type, and they want people to acknowledge their education and intelligence, especially when they are around women who have already made something of themselves and are perfectly balancing work and home. These educated but frustrated women keep comparing themselves with their other counterparts but are either too lazy or either too bookish actually to do something in the real world. These women keep wanting to do something and have ample time, but somehow their plans never materialize.

This category of women is always unhappy due to their constant dilemma of wanting to do something and lack of action. I know a woman who has discussed at least fifteen projects with me in detail pretty seriously over the past few years, but she hasn't started a single project. She makes a perfect project, is positive about it, is totally charged up and happy, and then boom, there goes her project in the air. She has this constant habit of making a fort and then blowing it up with dynamite of her negativity. Initially, I also felt very happy and excited for her every new project, but after she shelved her third project, I stopped taking any interest in her ventures because I have come to know that this woman is all sound and no show. The height is that this woman could feel all the unhappiness and frustration of a project going down just by planning it on paper. She hasn't tried a single thing or worked for a single day, but when she talks with someone, she speaks as if she is a failed entrepreneur.

I am sorry to say but two out of five women today belong to this category. They try to create a happy world for themselves, but they never try hard enough or realistically enough to see through a project, which leads to too much unhappiness in their and their family's lives. If you really can't just sit without doing anything, get up and do it. Just talking about something can only give you frustration and not happiness. So decide once and for all what you want from your life.

We all strive for happiness but remember happiness can never be achieved alone. Learn about the things that make your husband, your children, extended family, and friends happy. Also, be vocal in front of others about what makes you happy because no one is the magician to understand your desires. So speak up for your happiness. At the same time, be aware of the sparks that can fuse happiness in your relationship and be clever enough to incite a short circuit. It doesn't matter whether it's your family life or your professional life both hold the potential to make you more happy and satisfied but remember happiness is made, and no one can make you happy but yourself.

Acknowledgements

*I am thankful to my mother for all her love and guidance. I would have been nothing without her.

*I am thankful to my little angel, who keeps asking me, "mama, why aren't you writing today?" and keeps pushing me towards my art.

*I am thankful to my best friend Bhawna Chadha for always reading my first drafts and giving her honest opinion. Bhawna is also the first person always to like my posts, no matter which social platform it is. I am lucky to have a friend like her in my life and thank her from the cores of my heart for all the positivity she keeps instilling in me.

*I am thankful to my old gold friend Trupti Dekhne for reading my initial draft and criticizing it like a professional, which encourages me to improve my writing.

*I am thankful to my all ears friend Suman Kapoor for always giving her valuable insights and suggestions regarding my books.

*I am thankful to Utkarsh Chadha for proofreading the book and making it more reader-friendly.

*I am thankful to all my readers who have given so much love to my first book 'Surviving Mother & Mother-in-law, 'which motivated me to pen my second book.

*I thank the reader who has picked up a copy of Nobody has a Perfect Husband.I hope you enjoyed reading it as much as I enjoyed writing it.

*I thank my friends who shared their invaluable stories and experiences with me, without which this book wouldn't have been possible.May this book act as a guiding light for the men and women and enable them with wisdom to make their marriage a happy union.